Not Without My Mother's Boots

A Ukrainian Farmer's Memoir

Written by Nicholas Chrustie
Edited by b. christie

LIGHT SWITCH
PRESS

Published by:
Light Switch Press
PO Box 272847
Fort Collins, CO 80527

ISBN: 978-1-953284-88-4
Printed in the United States of America

My name is Nicholas, my father's name was Paul, and my mother's name was Maria. There was six of us in the family, three boys and three girls. The eldest was fourteen years old and the youngest was a one-year-old when we came to Canada. After one year in Canada, I had four sisters, totaling seven children.

I was born in 1892 in the village of Kolodiyiwka, Skalat district, in the constituency of Ternopol in Western Ukraine. At that time Ukraine was under Austrian rule king Franz Josef **1**.

Both of my parents were orphans. My mother's father passed away when my mother was ten years old. My father's mother passed away when my father was eight years old. They both worked for a living (that's their story).

After my parents got married, my mother got a half acre of land from her mother. My father had none so he was working for a landlord who had over a thousand acres of land and about five hundred acres of bush land meadows. This was mostly hardwood timbers such as oak, hickory, and big walnut trees. There were big orchards of apples, apricots, with several kinds of cherries, pears, plums, and many berries. But no one could pick one to eat as the orchids were always guarded.

My father was getting twenty-eight dollars a year in wages, four loads of fuel which was mostly underbrush – brush and willows- to keep the house warm, one bag which they called "koretz" (Four bushels) of corn, two 'koretz '(eight bushels) of rye, two 'koretz' of barley and buckwheat.

While my parents were living in the landlord's clay shack under the straw roof, they had a clay stove which was built in the shape of a half barrel. When the stove got hot during the day, it kept the room warm all night, but you had to cover all the windows and doors with the rye straw mats that were purposely made for the winter. It was braided out of the rye straw. Many people use to get sick from smoke inhalation and didn't know why.

The village had over fifteen hundred families, no doctor or hospital, two big churches – one catholic and one orthodox, four priest, and one policeman. The police use to carry a five foot rifle with a bayonet on the end. I remember that very well, as he used to come our way about once a week, and if we were playing on the streets and saw him from a distance we would run like "a rabbit when he sees a dog" and dodge into the shrubs or behind the fences until the police passed by. In our country, most of the land was good, but the landlords and churches owned it. The people had poorer land.

There was only one water well on each street for about seventy-five to a hundred families. There wasn't a fire brigade. The roofs of the houses were covered with flat bundles of rye straw, so, whenever a fire started on one side of the street with the wind in line, they couldn't stop it from burning to the end of the street. However, the walls of the houses never burned down as they were heavily plastered with clay. As soon as the fire started, especially at night, they would ring the bells on the churches as an alarm of caution. The busy would get busy and carry out everything they had in the house, so it wouldn't burn, such as clothing and furniture. They didn't have much furniture – one big chest like a big trunk, a table, no chairs only two or three benches about six feet long and a couple of smaller benches. I had never seen a chair until I stayed in a hotel at the seaport of Antwerp in Belgium. We stayed there three days waiting for a steamboat on our way to Canada.

The year I was born, I was told, my parents decided to build their own house. They moved from the landlord's house and the landlord gave them four dollars a year higher wages. He also permitted them to buy a cow and keep it in his stable using his feed in the winter and his pasture in the summer. Everyone who worked for the landlord for five years or more, and had two or three children were entitled to buy a cow if he could afford one. Otherwise, the women use to go a half mile to milk the landlord's cows for which they were allowed to take home one quart of milk. The landlord had eighty-five to ninety cows the year round for milking.

We lived about a half mile from the landlord's establishment (Headquarters) which was about a twenty-to-twenty-five-acre yard on which stables, granaries and workshops etc. were built. He had a larger number of horses, cattle, pigs, and poultry.

In those days, everyone worked from sunrise to sunset.in the wintertime, they worked from six a.m. to seven p.m. No one ever had breakfast in the morning until they did their morning chores then they were aloud to have what they called dinner. Those that had their own homes had wives taking dinner to them wherever they were working. The others were boarding at the landlords kitchen in which they were paying.

Thank God, we don't have to work now without breakfast, until ten or eleven a.m. or a woman having to take dinner to a man wherever he is working.

When I was four years old, I got cold sores around my mouth, it got so bad that I could not open my mouth to eat. And so, my mother went to some woman witch doctor. The woman advised my mother to make a salve (ointment) out of chimney soot, sulfur and fat grease, my mother put it on my sores, and I got blood poisoning. It went into my face, and it swelled up like a balloon and I couldn't see anything. "I remember that as yet!" Mother tried to get some one with a horse and wagon to take me to a doctor in the city of Skalat. There were no buggies in those days. Mother couldn't get anyone because it was the beginning of summer and everyone was busy. The next day she wrapped me in a bedspread like a rag and took a small piece of corn-flower, rye Bannock, and a jug of water and started carrying me to a doctor who was about six miles away. The weather got hot towards noon. I was sweating from being all wrapped up and mother was too. About every half mile she stopped and unwrapped me and cooled herself. She gave me a drink of warm water, there was no cold water along the road. No one lived about four miles and after getting to the place, mother got some fresh water and soaked the Bannock in it for me as I couldn't open my mouth to take a bite. I could then see a little with my right eye. When we got to the doctor, he cut my boils open. There were lumps around my left eye. He gave me some salve (medicine) and told us to go home. After a couple of hours, I had less pain. I walked with mother leading by the hand. We got home about sunset. I still have scares on my face, under the eyes where the doctor operated. I'll never forget it. Thank goodness I didn't lose my eye.

When it comes to harvest time, mother, like so many other people who had no land, used to help others cut the grain. She usually went to my father's place where my father was working. She would cut rye and wheat with a sickle. People were cutting grain for one sheaf out of every ten sheaves. They had to do this, because what other grain they did have was not enough when there were children to feed. The people had to make their own tie bands out of rye straw and had to take it with them every day to tie up the sheaves. They had to be the same size as you didn't know which sheaf you were going to get after it was cut and stocked. The field foreman used to come and count them out. There were thirty sheaves to one stock.

After harvest, they would get their sheaves home, and thresh them with a flail. Then the plate was ground by a two-plate hand operated stone grinder and later made into bread. For the barley we used to have a foot hopper operated by foot and you would hull the barley in it and make pot barley. For the buckwheat we also used the stone -plate grinder.

The barley and buckwheat were cut with a hand scythe. The men use to cut during the day and the women tied during the night so it wouldn't shell out too much.

I remember very well one day we had no bread or potatoes, only a piece of Bannock. Grandma used to look after me when mother was away working. It was sunset and we started to cry because we were hungry; there was no fresh water. Mother would leave us a wooden pail full of water to do us all day, so, towards evening that water got warm. Sorry! There was no ice pop like now.

Grandma told us, not to cry, as soon as the sun will get out of sight, and the moon will come out and mother will come home and get us something to eat. We sat around grandma on the bench and asked Grandma, "What is that moon?" grandma told us, "It is a big hole made by God in heaven, to light the earth so people could see how to bind the barley and buckwheat at night. That hole is made in the wall of heaven, but inside of it, it is very bright." Everyone who is good will go there and live with God because that's where God, and all the angels are. Grandma truly believed this. Today, about seventy years later, people have found out, that the moon is no hole but a planet. We learned, we must go further than that, to get to heaven. I think that story was made for the poor people. All the rich people have haven here.

First thing I knew, our cow had a calf. This was in the springtime of the year. Mother brought the calf home and put it in another room in our house as our house had two rooms. The room that had the stove was used in the winter only.

We had one bed made from lumber, no mattresses, only straw. About every month or so when the straw got to dry and all crushed, mother burned it in the stove and used fresh long straw again. There were no lumber floors, the children slept on the dirt floor with straw. The straw was covered in canvas sheets. The same kind of sheets were used for covers since there were no quilts. During the winter mother use to cover us with sheep skins over our coats. Some people had feather quilts.

During the summer, the fleas and lice got so bad that the floor had to be plastered almost every week and the walls were whitewashed with lime. It probably wasn't as bad with people who had side buildings or stables. Mother had to comb our heads and burn the lice in the stove.

Later, my father built an extension on to the house and used it for a storeroom and stable. Before that, mother kept about a dozen hens and one rooster in the attic. During the day, she would bring them down to feed. I think that is where we were getting the lice.

The roosters were kept chiefly for an alarm clock. He used to crow every hour before midnight. There were no clocks. If the rooster crowed one too many times, we could only blame the rooster for getting up to early.

That spring, as soon as the grass started to grow, mother would send my brother Mike, and me, to pick grass for the calf. We had to go on the meadow roads and along the creaks to get grass, we had to be back before mother had to take the dinner to dad. There was four of us boys and one sister. The oldest brother wasn't very healthy, mother didn't send him any place. Just brother Mike and me. Suddenly the older brother caught a cold and a fever and died, then we got a baby boy, brother Peter. This made the fourth boy. Brother Mike started to go to school and got sick. The weather was cold in December. Mother went to the priest and the teacher to beg them to release Mike from school. Due to the circumstances and hardship, my parents couldn't buy clothing or boots. There were no shoes at that time, only high boots, no socks or stockings. Everyone used cotton rag strips for wrapping around the feet or used long straw tucked in the boots.

The following fall of 1899, my mother had to send me to school. During the warm weather, the first year, the children went to school in the afternoon only. When the weather got cold with snow on the ground, mother put her boots on my feet and a lot of rags inside. The boots were to big for me, it was hard to walk. I walked slowly and got used to them, so I could run in them a little. Mother told me not to skate in them, we walked along the creek where there was ice. The other kids used to skate, and one day I tried too. Mother found out from the neighbors, and she gave me an awful thrashing and I couldn't sit with my full seat on the bench for a few days. There were no chairs or desks in the school, only one low long bench to write on.

After Christmas, the snow got very deep, I couldn't go to school every day. I could only go when mother let me use her boots after dinner. The teacher promoted me to the second grade with morning and afternoon classes because I had no boots or clothing, I could only continue afternoon classes in second grade.

One cold day, mother put her overcoat on me, it was extremely long, she folded double up to my underarms and tied it with a cotton belt about four inches wide. When I got to school the teacher helped me undress. After school, the teacher put the overcoat on me the same way and I started for home, which was a "Canadian mile."

I had to walk home, rather slowly with that big coat on, halfway home, I felt an emergency to go to the bathroom. There were no bushes or places I could hide along the road. I was bashful, I tried to walk faster and the first thing I knew, I had my pants full, and a lot of it slid into my boots and I started to cry. It so happened, a woman was coming along the road and asked me my name. After some time, I told her, and she took my hand. She told my mother not to whip me. At the end of the second year, the teacher promoted me to a higher class "B."

During the summer, I was often gazing other people's geese, sheep, and was getting eight cents a day. Mother bought me boots that were my size and a coat. Then I was able to go to school from morning to evening. I was taking a lunch with me, which was two potatoes one day, rye Bannock the next day and buckwheat buns.

I finally got acquainted with one of the boys who lived on our street. He had been going to school for four years and was still in grade one. One evening he invited me to his place. His mother asked if I liked going to school and asked what grade I was in? She couldn't believe I was doing so well. She asked me to help her boy and she gave me a slice of bread, about two inches across the loaf (the old country loafs were about three-to-four-pound size) and a four-inch square piece of pork fat. And I took that home and my mother was glad. Mother rendered the pork that evening and greased our pea soup which was incredibly good. I still remember how good it was! We never had pork, only hemp oil.

Hemp is something like flax, only it is much bigger. It grows four to five feet tall. When it is threshed, it is about the size of a tapioca. They made oil out of the seed and took the fibre out of the straw with wire brushes and then spun it into a thread to make white material which was like a light canvas. They used this to make pants and shirts. The women would dye the material to make skirts.

I was helping my friend out almost every day, I had a lot of bread for lunches the rest of the year. One day, the teacher caught me doing his work, and I got three whippings across my seat, after that, I had to be careful. The next year, I moved to a different room, it was a three room school. I lost my friend.

I still remember when the teacher told us to write January 2, 1900. That spring, mother's brother went to Canada. My mother got a letter from him. She had to go to the municipal secretary to have the letter read to her. She had to pay ten cents for having the letter read and ten cents for having the letter written.

At the end of the school season, I passed my grade with honours, and I started reading my uncles letters and started writing to him. My uncle settled in Gimli, Manitoba.

The next year, I was in grade four but couldn't go to school, because of the cold weather and no warm clothing. Mother used to report that I was sick. So, I was lucky that I passed to grade four.

The winters were only about three months long. The snow goes away in March and April. Every- thing is blooming- orchards, maples, the birds are coming back- cuckoos singing "cuckoo cuckoo." The big white storks rattling on the rooftops. The bees start working. You never forget this.

During the summer, I went around grazing other people's cows and geese. This wasn't too bad, but when the grain crops started to head, the landlord hired children to weed the crops. The fifty to seventy children would spread out into a wide row and walk up and down the fields until all the weeds were pulled out. When you hit a patch of thistles or nettles and pull them without gloves it wasn't pleasant. By evening, your fingers were swelled up and sore that you couldn't hold a spoon at suppertime.

After the crops were taken off, we use to go on the landlords' fields to pick the grain heads out of the stubble and took them home to dry. Then we would shell them out, ground them and make Bannock. This would last only if the weather was dry, otherwise, it sprouts and is no good for making flour.

After that summer mother got sick. A couple of days went by and then father went to the boss (Landlords manager) and begged him for a team of horses to take mother to a doctor. The doctor diagnosed her with typhoid fever. Mother had to stay in bed for two to three weeks. Father could not take her to a hospital because he had no money. Father couldn't get anyone to look after mother, so he asked the boss if he could put me in his place, for my father to stay home. The boss granted him leave of absence, and sent me to work with two other men grazing sixty to seventy head of milk cows. That morning dad got me out of bed, gave me a couple of potatoes (baked) and a piece of bread. I left the house in the dark. When I got to the stable it was getting daylight. The women were finishing milking the cows by hand. The foreman came and told us to chase the cows out. There was another boy, about five or six years older than me and a lot bigger. One had to go on each side of the road and the foreman kept chasing the cows until we got them to the pasture. We took them out of the stubble fields until the fields were plowed.

In the mornings there was heavy dew on the ground, so, I had to keep busy to keep warm for I didn't have shoes. After a few days, my feet got chapped and sore, and started bleeding. They were worse around the ankles. When the foreman saw my feet, he promised we wouldn't have pasture the cows on the stubble anymore.

The boy with me, told me to wet my feet in urine, which I did, and nearly died with pain. I was jumping around like crazy; it was burning like fire. I started crying, and the foreman, who wasn't far away, heard me, and asked the other boy, what happened? The foreman than went and got a jug of water and told me to wash my feet. In a while I was better. The foreman gave me some axil grease to put on my feet every morning. The foreman was very good.

He used to give me some of his dinner every day. He was an elderly man, I believe. I ran all day watching the cows on his side and mine.

Two and a half weeks passed, and mother got better. I put in twenty days working, but the end of the month, dad didn't get paid for the days he was absent. The boss asked him "Do you expect a school boy to earn men's wages?" Which was about three dollars a month, plus the grain and corn. I ended up working for nothing. Father had promised me a pair of boots if I did my job well. I had to do without boots.

It isn't any wonder, people revolted in Russia and Poland. They suffered terribly hard times and slavery.

My mother's stepfather told us stories of him being in the army for twelve years. He was in different countries just like our armies are now in Germany, Korea and Vietnam etc. Mother's stepfather spoke four or five different languages. When he was released from the army he got sixty dollars pay (five dollars a year). He told us that during the slavery decade in Poland, each man had to work two days a week for nothing. If you went to work too early, you were blamed for wanting to steal something, you got three whippings on the "dupa" (butt). If you came too late, you would get three whippings for every half hour you were late. How would you like that for "yobkas" (apples)?

A couple of years later, my uncle from Canada, started insisting my parents move to Canada. He told them that they would get one hundred and sixty acres of land for ten dollars and they would at least have plenty of wood to keep the house warm. A year later, my parents decided to sell what property they had and everything else, except the clothing, bedsheets and the quilts.

In 1905, in the beginning of July, we started out for Canada. We travelled mostly by freight train. And we were glad we had some bedding or else we would have to sleep on the bare box car

floors. The train was especially crowded through Germany as many people were going to Canada, America, Argentina.

In about three or four days, we arrived at the seaport of Antwerp, in Belgium where we waited three days for a steamboat. It was the hotel in Antwerp that I saw chairs and tables for the first time. And tasted very good meals.

The fourth day, we got on the boat. The first and second days on the boat weren't bad, but the third day, the sea was very rough, and everyone got seasick. We were sick for two days. After twelve days on the boat, we arrived at Quebec City, that evening we got on the train and were in Montreal the next day. We had to wait a couple of hours for another train. We got to Toronto the next day and stayed a short while and then went on to Winnipeg. The immigration officer took us to the immigration hall which is still across the street from C.P.R.

station. The old C.P.R. station was small, but at that time they were working on a new building which still has the imprint 1905 on it.

The first night in Winnipeg, we slept on the floor. The second day, we got some old mattresses and no one could sleep that night because of bed bugs. Mostly everyone got up and walked around all night. The next morning, the mattresses were shown to the immigration officer. They were full of bugs, like an ant pile. He laughed and we never used the mattresses again.

Mother asked the immigration officer to notify my uncle, the next day we received a letter from him telling us to come to Winnipeg beach as there was no train to Gimli.

When we arrived at Winnipeg Beach, uncle was there with a neighbor who had a team of horses to take us to his place which was fourteen miles away. My uncle only had a team of oxen. My uncle had a log house with two rooms. We spent two weeks there then moved to a log shack twelve by sixteen. It had two lumber bunk beds with hay mattresses on which the smaller children slept and three of us on the floor where we put up for four years. We only had a box iron back stove heater on which mother cooked all the time and, a clay country style stove was built outside for baking bread.

That summer, we helped uncle put up some hay as he had two oxen, six cows, and four calves. All the hay had to be cut with a hand scythe. After haying father and uncle went out to work harvesting and we worked around the yard. We went to the bush and picked cranberries for making jam for winter. We then went around helping different people dig potatoes. We were paid with potatoes. Mother was getting a bushel of potatoes a day and I was getting a half a bushel. We had to carry those potatoes home on our backs every night in the dark. Some of the places were three miles away and it was very hard going through bush trails. Mother use to talk loudly when we go to the big timber bushes because she was afraid of black bears and wolves. There were many around. Many times, I cried on the way home, because I was tired.

After the potato digging was over, we started carrying in dry poles of wood from the bush and box sawed them by hand for the winter supply.

Around the beginning of November, the men came home from harvesting. If the harvest season was good, they worked thirty to thirty-five days with wages of a dollar and seventy-five cents for stooking and two dollars and twenty-five cents for threshing. After work, harvesting with brother Mike, we had to go and catch bush rabbits with sticks, so we had meat, before it got too cold. Father had a hard time getting a job the first year because he couldn't speak English. He only made forty dollars that season. When he got home, father bought a few groceries and couldn't buy winter clothing for us to go to school which was two miles away.

Once freeze up came we got a job threshing grain- barley, oats and buckwheat on the icy ground. We were getting fifty cents a day and were able to buy some winter clothes. We also cut cord wood at fifty cents a cord.

The following year mother sent me out to work for the priest's wife. I had to baby sit a two year old boy, look after four cows, two calves and one horse. She had a buggy for summer travelling and a cutter (sleigh) for the winter. She used to pay mother twenty – five dollars a year or two dollars a month if I didn't stay a year. Working wasn't too bad, but I would get home sick. There was always something to eat and the lady was good to me. In the wintertime, she gave me her husband's size ten or eleven, knew high boots to wear while doing the outside chores.

One day, in the spring the lady told me to harness the horse for her and hitch him to the cutter. She told me to play nicely with the boy and watch the stove fires and she would ask mother to send my brother to stay with me. Our house was a half a mile away. After my brother came around, my brother started playing and decided to see what was in the kitchen cupboard. This lady had a shotgun, so we found some gun powder and twelve-gauge brass shells. We didn't know how to make the gun shoot so we filled the gun shells about half full of powder and I told my brother to put it on the stove. But he was smarter and told me not to because it might blow the roof of the kitchen. My brother told me to take some hot coals outside, and I did. Mike put the shells half full of powder on the ground and walked a few feet away. Then I went with the hot coals up to the shell and a big fire exploded and burnt the left side of my face, eye, and half my hair. "I yelled like crazy!" I bumped my head in the snow, as I was in terrible pain. I wanted to run home but couldn't see because I swelled up like a balloon in no time. I tried to open my right eye with which I could see a little. I ran half naked, a half mile to Auntie's place but mother wasn't home. Auntie sent for mother. My mother and father came running. The lady sent Mike home and father nearly killed poor Mike. Whipping him with a half inch rope, until he fainted.

That fall, we got another sister, Ann. That following winter, mother told me to try and teach all of the kids- two brothers and three sisters – to read and write, in the Ukrainian language. I did, and I was able to get them all to read and write in the language.

In the spring, the priest came home and hired us to clear some land for him. Whoever had a homestead, was supposed to live on it three years, clear and cultivated five acres of land, before he could get title to it.

The following fall, my uncle went to look at a new homestead which was opened about forty miles north of Gimli. There were no railroads, so they went out walking on a bush trail. We planned to settle all together on more open land. He took a homestead for my dad.

I got a job with an Icelandic farmer, as mother wanted me to go to work where I could learn to speak English as a lot of Icelanders spoke English. Father bought me a Ukrainian -English dictionary and I started to study the English language. This Islander offered to pay me four dollars a month or fifty dollars a year.

I started to work there in November. There were two boys, one was ten and the other was twelve. I had good company when they were at home, they were going to school. Their father was working at the town of Gimli and I was at home late in the evening and went away early in the morning with a horse and cutter (one horse sleigh).

I was looking after twenty-two head of cattle and milking four cows, morning and evening. I bucked saved all the wool for two stoves – a cook stove and a big wood heater. I pumped all the water for the cattle and shoveled snow after every storm. The worst of it all was that the old Icelander, use to wake me up every morning at six o clock, but his boys were aloud to sleep longer. I had to go out with a coal- oil lantern to feed the cattle hay, and milk the cows, then I would go in to eat breakfast. However, there was a lot to eat; milk, bread, and lots of fish. There wasn't much meat or eggs. In a couple of months, I could speak English and Icelandic. About the middle of April, my father took me away from my work at the Icelanders to go with him to find that homestead because he couldn't speak English.

My father sold his farm, and instead of going on the homestead with my father as planned, he decided to go west to Alberta. He told my father to go find his homestead and a lot of arguments started and that is why my father took me away from work to go as an interpreter.

April is usually nice weather. Mother made some cottage cheese and butter mixture and father took two loaves of bread and on a nice sunshiny morning we started out on the forty-five mile walk to our homestead. We walked along lake Winnipeg, as that was the only road (horse trail). It was called fish road because they use to bring the fish to Gimli on it. They got the railroad to to Gimli that year. This was in 1908 and we started to go north in the spring of 1909. It was good walking in the morning, but in the afternoon the snow became soft and wet. We only had leather shoes and our feet got wet by the afternoon.

We got to the homestead the next day towards evening. The nearest farmer (Icelander) was three miles from the homestead and I asked if we could stay overnight (and we did). The next morning, we went to see the land. We stayed the next night with the Icelandic farmer again and the following day we started back for Gimli.

At eight in the morning, as usual, it was all frozen and good walking. About noon it got sloppy again, we got away about twelve miles and I was getting hungry. We came by one farmer, and I went to the house and asked if we could get something to eat. The lady gave us some fish and potatoes for lunch. We started out along the river on a graded road which was sticky with mud and heavy walking. Towards evening, after sunset, I was getting hungry again and tired and couldn't see any farmhouses along the way. Suddenly, we noticed a house in the bush. We went to the yard, and a dog started barking. There wasn't a light in the house, and they only used a stovepipe hole to light the house when they were sitting and knitting mitts and socks out of wool yarn. Most of the people kept cattle and sheep and made their own sweaters, mitts and socks and sold what they did not need. After we got closer to the house a man came out. I told him we were hungry and asked him for a meal. He invited us into the house and the lady got some potatoes that were cooked in their skin, skinned them and put them in a pan with some tallow.

She asked me if we liked moose meat, and I told her that we have never tasted it before. She said it's like beef. So, we had potatoes, moose meat and skimmed milk. We thanked them for the supper and started out for home. After walking about an hour, I got an upset stomach. Then, I got diarrhea and more than my supper was out of me in a couple of hours, and I was weaker than before supper.

We finally arrived in Gimli around twelve thirty a.m. There were no lights on in any of the few houses that were in the town of Gimli at that time. There was a light in the hotel, and we went there and dad got a small bottle of whisky from the night watchmen for fifty cents. In those days, you could buy liquor at any time of the day and the price was five dollars a galloon. Dad told me to take a little drink and in no time I fell asleep. But instead of letting me sleep for awhile, my dad woke me up by saying "Lets go, lets go!" I went outside and got chills like a convulsion. He told me to run, which I tried and after awhile I was warmed up. We came home, which was five miles from Gimli, when it started getting daylight. As soon as I hit the inside warmth of the house, I dropped and fainted. Mother was scared. They worked on me for, I don't know how long till they brought me to life and lifted me off the floor and put me in bed until I stayed until the next day before I could get up myself. And that was the first homestead trip.

After the snow was gone, my father got a team of oxen from my uncle for helping him on the farm for four years. We had two cows and two calves. Father took me and Mike and we went to the homestead with the team of oxen and the wagon. In the two days we were there started to haul logs for the buildings. We built a house and a stable (it was a two-room house). Since we had no money to buy shingles, we covered the roof with hay bundles under which we lived for seven years, then we changed to shingles, and that house was still there, to which we built another room.

Father was able to get another job in the bush. I got a job too, at a farmer's, for fifteen dollars a month. I had to milk four cows every morning before going to work, and every night after coming home from work.

After a couple of weeks working, putting up hay for the winter, the weather got very hot. Pushing hay in the bush valley was very hot and I was sweating all the time and drinking warm water with rolled oats in it. There was no coco cola nor orange crush in those days. Anyways, I got inflammation in my eyes from the sweat, and I couldn't see anything. I had to quit the job. After a couple of days, I went with mother two miles to the neighbor. I had to go because my mother couldn't speak a word of English. We got a horse and buggy from the neighbor, and she took me to a doctor sixteen miles away. We started out about nine a.m. and we were home about eleven p.m. that day. The doctor gave me some medicine and told me what to do to stay away from the sun and light for three weeks. I did get better.

After that I did not go out working. I was helping mother to dig clay and mixing it with cut up hay, we plastered the log buildings.

In the winter I went out working with a farmer, looking after thirty head of cattle (as a chore boy) and had to milk six cows. The farmer's wife was sick for over a month, and I had to do all the outside work alone. Later, she helped me milk the cows as her husband was away working at the sawmill. In the spring, when he got home, he told me to go home.

In the middle of May, I got a job with land surveyors. They were paying thirty-five dollars a month. I thought, oh boy, it won't be long, and I'll be a rich man. But when the weather got hot, the flies got very bad. Mosquitos; bulldog flies; flying ants; and blackflies were all after your blood. Ever since then I couldn't forget how good was our lord that created all those insects to suck your blood and make you curse and swear. And it didn't matter how religious a person was. Later, when the water in the swamps and muskeg got stale and your feet were wet all day and every day, your feet were inflamed and scalded like boiling water on them. Most of the men were lying in their tents (camps) like babies. After it heals up, you are alright for the rest of the season.

One man from New Zealand, was very sick with scalded feet and after he got better, he quit the job. Another man from Windsor, Ontario decided to quit before he got sick. Brother Mike and I decided to quite and go home with them as we were planning to help dad put up hay for the cattle. And all the hay had to be put up by hand and cut with hand scythes. We told the chief engineer that we were quitting the job and we got paid. That was in the evening. The next morning we started out for home with the New Zealander and the man from Windsor. We had to walk thirty-four miles to our home and they had to walk thirty-eight miles before they could get to the first P.O. by the name of Geysir which is still on the map. It was all through bush and swamp on a winter fish hauling trail. The nearest house was twenty-six miles away which we thought we could reach before dark with no trouble. We knew of those people, as they were eight miles east of my father's homestead. The weather was very hot, and we were in the swamp for a half a mile or more and then in the bush for a couple of miles. We made about twenty-five miles. We had lunch, enough for the whole day. In the last swamp we were crossing before that house the man from Windsor got sick halfway through. There were bushes here and there and we lead him to the nearest one. He laid down and yelled and cried like a sick pig. None of us could carry him out as we were getting tired, we had baggage of our own to carry. In the morning, twenty five or forty pounds wasn't heavy but after all day on your shoulders in the hot weather it was like three or four hundred pounds. I decided to go out on high bush land which was a couple of hundred yards and I found water under a spruce tree. I made tea with the water. I ate lunch and drank a cup of tea and went back to give the sick man a drink of tea. When I arrived at the swamp, I met them. I gave the sick man a drink and took his luggage. We took him, to where the fire was, where I made the tea and we sat there until sunset. Then the mosquitos got busy and wanted to take more blood to heaven. Anyways, we didn't curse anymore as that Windsor man with sore feet did all the cursing and swearing. Slowly, I carried the two sets of luggage and my brother and the New Icelander helped the sick man to walk, and we arrived at the homestead house in the edge of dark.

The people were home, and we asked them if we could stay there overnight. They only had a one room shack. The lady said she was sorry, but she didn't have enough bedding for four. We told her we had our own blankets, and happy to be away from the mosquitos, we could rest a little on the floor. The man went outside and brought in a big bundle of hay and spread it over the floor. We spread out our blankets and in no time I fell asleep.

I don't know how long I slept. I woke up and saw my three partners sitting up with a candle and whispering something. I sat up to see what they were looking at and saw one solid mass of fleas running around like ants in an ant pile. One guy said, "We've jumped out of a frying pan into a fire." The Windsor man said, "If we feed all those fleas with our blood, will have no blood left, that's for sure." We decided to go outside and make a smudge to keep the mosquitos away and try to rest. We picked our blankets up and left the people in the house snoring away like nobody's business. When we exited the house, we saw a stable not too far from the house. We went to it and as the night was getting cooler, the mosquitos were not too bad. We took some hay to the stable and went to sleep there. We slept to the guy came and called us for breakfast.

We went into the house, and the lady had a small table set with five small dishes full of porridge, milk, coffee and three small buns made from rolled oats and flour. Most people use to make them that way when they were short of flour. The lady ate her porridge out of the pot. The buns were cut in half, but we had some of our sandwiches which we ate with coffee, although they were already dry.

We were ready to go, as we left the house, the farmer walked with us bidding us goodbye. The Windsor man stepped to the side and touched a small pile of saw dust, which was about a foot deep, a couple of yards from the house door. In no time, he looked and jumped about three feet high and shouted, "Jesus Christ!!" when we looked at the saw dust pile, it was a solid mass of fleas. We told the farmer that he should burn it up because that is where the fleas were hatching but he said, "They don't bother him." We said, "goodbye to our partners." They went south and we went west, to get to our home, but both men said, "Goodbye to Manitoba."

We arrived home about noon. It was very hot, and we only had a quarter to drink. Our parents were glad to see us home. Father had already started cutting hay. The next day, we got busy, two of us cutting with scythes. Mother and the girls were raking hay with hand rakes, which were made of wood, about two and a half feet wide. After they had raked, we started stacking. After we finished the haying, we started harvesting.

We went to find harvest work near Winnipeg, but when we got to Winnipeg, we found it hard to find work there. We went to the unemployment office, and we signed up to go to Cypress River, which is 105 miles west of Winnipeg.at that time, they were taking harvest labourers for one cent a mile and it cost us three dollars for the three of us and we were told at the unemployment centre that it was all big farmers, and they needed a lot of men. The next day we got onto the train and arrived at Cypress River about noon. The town was not big, about thirty to forty-five houses, one hardware store, one dry goods and grocery store, one big church, a grain elevator and a C.P.R. with about a fifty-foot-long platform. And on that platform was all about fifty men looking for jobs. We went to the grocery store to get some things for lunch. We got five cents worth of tea and sugar, three tins of sardines and one loaf of bread. We could only get one loaf because the storekeeper couldn't sell anymore, and he told us he had lots of "Sea tack." We got five pounds of hard sea tack at five cents a pound. Sea tack is made of flour like Bannock.

We required about work, but no one wanted more men until threshing, which was expected to start the following week, and this was a Tuesday. We didn't get a job that day, we bought more sardines and made tea on a campfire. We slept in a box car, and the next morning we had the same thing for breakfast. After breakfast, we talked to the storekeeper, and he phoned someone for us, who wanted men to stack grain sheaves on a farm, about five miles away. We walked there, only to find the farmer only wanted two men to pitch sheaves which is extremely hard work, from seven a.m. to seven p.m., one hour for lunch, for two dollars and twenty-five cents a day. He didn't hire me and my brother, as he didn't think we could handle the job.

We didn't stop there. We started back to town on a different road and called on the farmers along the way but got no job. The day was hot, and after the tack and sardine breakfast, I was hungry. I went to a farmhouse and a lady answered my knock at the door. I told her we were looking for jobs and we were hungry and would like to buy a loaf of bread.

But she said, "Sorry, this is not a bakery shop." And slammed the door in my face. We tried one more house for a loaf of bread, but with the same results. We arrived in time about four p.m. and bought more hard tack. We made tea and had a piece of cheese and that was our dinner and supper. There were still a lot of men coming, looking for jobs. Several of them came as far east as Nova Scotia because the harvest fare was cheap, one cent a mile.

Towards evening the C.P.R. station agent came out and told us not to sleep in the C.P.R. boxcars because the police would be coming later and would prosecute us. We went out a quarter of a mile into a grain field where the grain was cut and stooked. We made a bed out of sheaves and built a three walled shelter. We had our own blankets. After dark, we went to sleep, and when you walk all day and are tired, you soon fall asleep. A man that was with us woke up and started yelling "Get up, get up!!" A storm was coming, we got up and could hear loud rough thunder not far from us, a strong wind started to blow. We picked up our blankets and baggage (spare clothes) and started to run towards town to get under the shelter of a boxcar or the elevator, so we wouldn't get wet. We had only about fifty or sixty more yards to go but couldn't run anymore. The rain and hail caught us, and it poured down. It wasn't long before we were soaking wet. We got under the elevator, but the wind and draft were strong and in no time we were shivering from the chill. After a short time, the rain stopped, and we went to the side of the building. The sun was coming out and we took off our clothes, rubbing ourselves with the dry parts of the blankets. We pulled out dry clothes from the flour bags we carried them in, for there were no suitcases in those days.

It became warmer with the sun shining again and we made our breakfast. We found an old syrup can and made our tea in it. We went to the store and this time; we were able to get another loaf of bread. We also got a dozen eggs and boiled them. "Oh boy, did we ever have a big meal that day."

We kept walking around town, and as soon as we saw a farmer coming to town, we rushed over and tackled him down, for a job, but unfortunately, farmer's come into town, to do their own shopping. The first farmer said, "he didn't need any men. In a few minutes, we saw another farmer coming (we were on the outskirts of town) and asked him. He said, "he would need four or five men in two or three days when he would begin threshing. I can still remember his name was Jas. He said, "If you fellows like to come to my place and do some work around the yard until I'm ready, "I'll give you board and room free." He told us where he lived, four miles from town, and we said, "We would go." We started for his place and arrived around noon. We found a man in his yard, working there all summer. He told us that they would have been threshing already, but a sad thing had happened. There had been a funeral the day before, the farmers only son, passed away suddenly on the road going to town.

In a little while the boss got home and told us to go to the caboose (small shack on wagon wheels) where the threshing gang stayed and cleaned it up and put fresh hay in the bunk beds, there were no mattresses. Just as we started, he called us in for dinner. We had a good dinner, expressed our sympathy at the loss of their son and the lady was kind of glad that we sympathized.

After dinner, we asked him if there was anything special, he would like us to do. He asked if we came from the city or a farm. I told him I came from a small farm (homestead). He said there is a big pile of wood to split and pile for some fences to fix around the yard. We started at it and finished the next day. Then we started doing the fences. He was very satisfied. There was two of us fencing and two were fixing hay racks for stock wagons. On the fourth day, we started threshing.

We threshed for over three weeks. The threshing machine was big and was operated by a steam engine. He had his neighbors helping in the hauling of sheaves and after we threshed for them. Wherever threshing machine went, the caboose went too, and that farmer used to board the gang.

We moved to his neighbors a couple of miles away. His name was Scott, who I'll never forget. While threshing the grub (board) wasn't too bad though very seldom we get more than one egg (in an egg cup) and a bowl of porridge for breakfast. We also got green tea which I wasn't used to drinking and I didn't get used to it and hated it. On Sunday, there was porridge only, no eggs. Dinner consisted of soup, one slice of bread and butter, syrup or a little dish of fruit. Supper, we had an onion sandwich, a little fruit and that stinking tea, even though we were helping him with the chores around the barn and yard, he never gave us any different meals.

After a couple of days of threshing, it rained and there was no threshing, but we always went out and did work around the yard, hoping we would get more to eat. Neither the woman nor man would put out anymore than a slice of bread for each of us.

We had a box stove wood heater in the caboose and on the wet evenings we lit a fire in it. We decided, rather than go to town to buy something to eat, we would take. About noon, we went to the stable and picked up all the eggs we could find. After dark, we went to the garden, and dug some potatoes and carrots. We would cook them at night and had always swiped enough salt from the table to cook with. So, we didn't have to starve anymore.

On Saturday nights, they use to go to town, and this Scott guy, was a stingy old devil, so we killed one of his young chickens and roasted it with potatoes and carrots. We had a good dinner, but we still had to go and eat his onion sandwiches, so he wouldn't be suspicious. We worked twelve to thirteen hours a day and had no lunch between meals.

The following winter, like a good many others, we started cutting cord wood. And now, we had two teams of oxen, but we were eight miles from town, and it took us two days with the two teams, and two of us in the bush to deliver two cords of tamarack wood (dry) which is very hard to cut. We got two dollars and twenty-five cents a cord. We quit and went to cut lumber logs on shares with an old Scotsman by the name of Cameron, who, before that had sawmill in Leifer, north of Amaranth (Harcus). He was the father of Mrs. Stanley of Amarath, who was still there. Bob was his son-in-law. They had moved their sawmill to Leifer to Arborg and during the moose hunting season. Cameron's son was killed by this companion hunter, both son-in – laws pulled out and the old man persuaded us to go in the lumber business with him, which he did.

The winter was mild and there was not much snow. We could not operate the mill as we couldn't get water for the steam engine, which was used to operate it. With the mill not operating, myself and two brothers were cutting logs. We built a small shack to live in. We brought most of the grub from home, but never had enough meat. One evening, my brother asked me to kill a moose. Early the next morning, around six a.m. when we got up, we had breakfast and went outside. There was a high south wind blowing, when I set out to hunt for a moose. I took a compass, rifle and knife with me, and told my brother approximately where I was going, and left around daybreak. I walked about a mile and a half and came upon fresh moose track. The wind was still strong, and it had rained and snowed a little. That was January 22, 1913. I followed the tracks a few hundred yards and came to an opening on little ridge, where it looked like a fire had gone through, as most of the trees were broken, and brush started to grow. I looked to the side and here was a big moose getting off the ground. He had been lying about fifty yards from me. In no time I had my gun up and fired a shot. The moose bellowed loud and dropped to the ground. I looked to the other side and here was another one, but this one was further away, and running at full speed. I fired two shots at the other one, but he went into the brush, and I didn't see him anymore. I started going towards the first one, where he was lying down. I got close to home, and could see that he had his head up, chomping with his mouth wide open. I wanted to grab him by his horns to turn him down and cut his neck to bleed him out, but had no room, but had no room because he was lying near a big log. I was stupid for not firing another shot in his head, as I was stingy about a ten-cent shell. I wanted to go around him and grab him from the other side. I couldn't get around behind him, I walked in front with my rifle loaded. I thought if he ever moves, I'll fire again. He laid with his feet under him, and kept chomping with his mouth until I got right straight in front of him, when he suddenly jumped up on his feet and tried to grab me by the shoulders. I dodged as he hit me with his mouth, and I fell over a log that was nearby. I fell on one side of the log, and he fell on the other with one of his feet on top of it, and I didn't know where my rifle was. by looking at the moose, I couldn't breathe, and my heart was working like an old railroad steam engine. If I laid there for a minute, I must have laid there for half an hour before I could move. After I got cooled off, I started to move away from him. I lifted my head and saw my gun on the side of the log where the moose was lying. I worked myself away and got to the log again, and then crawled along it until I could reach my rifle and crawled away. My pants were wet from the snow. I cleared the wet snow from my rifle and blew the barrel out. I rose on my knees and still being shaky, fired two shoots into his head, but I was afraid to bleed him out immediately. I made a small fire to keep warm and dry my pants and then I started to skin him, and every time his muscles jumped, I jumped. I had him dressed and cut in half. after that, I wanted to see if I hit the other one that I shot at twice, as soon as I came upon his tracks I saw a trace of blood in the snow, and was scared, and decided to go back to camp.

I told my brothers, I hit a moose. My brother Mike, took a gun and came with me and a team of oxen, and we loaded the meat and he saw where the moose was lying and where I was. He went to look for the other moose, expecting he might be dead. He went out and I stayed with the oxen. In no time, I heard the shots fired. He kept shooting every few minutes, and fired fourteen of the fifteen shells he had and did not kill the moose. He came back and told me, he couldn't hit him and wanted me to go, as the moose was lying down every few hundred yards and getting up and dropping again. As he had one shell left, we both went and finished the moose off. We got two moose, but I couldn't sleep most of that night. Since then, I killed forty-five moose, but never took chances like that again.

Towards March, we received a lot of snow, and we started the mill. Mike was on the engine, and I was on the saw. We cut over forty thousand feet of lumber, but lumber was cheap and I couldn't move all the lumber away from the mill to home. In the spring, the "Case Machinery Company" came up to collect payment on the engine which wasn't completely paid and this Cameron had no money, the company seized all the lumber, his and ours too. We lost most of our winters work, for nothing.

The following summer, the first world war broke out, and many young men joined the army and went to Europe to kill other men like themselves. Millions of people, women and children died for nothing. The war didn't bring any good to the world, only disability and poverty. After four years of war, the Asian flu hit the world and in one year, it took more people's lives then four years of world war. After three days, a doctor arrived and told mother what to do to keep the fever down and thank God, we all came out of it alive. The flu hit in the fall of 1918.

After war and sickness, there was a bigger demand for labour, and better wages. The following spring, I went out to work on a farm near Killarney, Manitoba. I worked there seven months, and I purchased a team of young horses and shipped them home to Arborg. I had a little money left, as the horses cost me three hundred dollars, that was my wages for seven months work. I decided to buy myself, a suit, and clothes which I never had before. I bought a suit for twelve dollars and some other clothes, and a pair of dress shoes. I went home like a millionaire. It wasn't as if I was proud of it, but many fellows like me, were a little jealous.

Since the country was becoming well settled, and people were getting a little more acquainted, they started to have dance parties. One Sunday, I went with my brother Mike to a dance party. We had gone to several parties by this time, as he was a fiddler.

There were mostly young people at the dance, and, the first thing I knew, they started dancing, and a girl came up to me and invited me to dance with her. I was very shy, and I couldn't look at the girl, for I didn't know who she was. All I could say was, no, no, no! Another girl came and both grabbed me by the arms and pulled me into a dance ring. The dance room was small, and all the parties were held in the farm homes, most places had rough lumber floors. There were no hardwood floors then. One girl let go, and the other one hung on to me, showing me how to dance. I think I was dancing like a calf, when you take him outside for the first time on a rope. After a few parties, I started inviting girls myself to a dance, and got engaged to one of the girls, I went out with her for almost two years. Then I decided to go on the prairie farming. I went to Winnipeg, and found a place to rent a six hundred acre cultivated farm. My brother Peter and I and another guy, rented it out. I borrowed some money from my brother-in- law and went to Stowton, Saskatchewan and bought eleven horses, a tractor and more machinery, and we started farming on a big scale at Westbourne, Manitoba. The first year, we had a good crop. Prices were good after the war, wheat was two fifty to three dollars a bushel. After threshing, I paid most of my outside debts and had about a thousand dollars left over. I went back to Arborg and found out that my girl left me and married someone else. I was more excited from that than the bull moose that jumped on me. That upset me terribly, and then whatever I did, didn't seem enjoyable. Nobody knows the heartache I felt. That winter, I worked in the bush, and in the spring, went back on the prairie farm, as we rented it for three years, I told my brother to quit, but he wouldn't do it. The second summer, the government froze the price on wheat at one dollar a bushel, barley sixty-five cents, oats, forty cents, and the crop wasn't as good. Closer to harvest time, I went to Winnipeg to make arrangements to get twine for harvesting. On the second day, I found out a midnight passenger killed five of our horses, which had cost us about eleven hundred dollars. I had to buy four horses to harvest the crop, and in the fall just the barley cleared expenses. Brother Peter quit, but Mike insisted on staying on the farm for another year. One of my sisters, who was cooking for us, told me, that she was quitting, and to find another cook, which I did. In Arborg again, and during the winter, I worked in the bush. In the meantime. I found a cook and married her on March the 11th in 1921. And she continued to cook for me. After we got married, we moved to Westbourne to the prairies farm.

After a year on that big farm, we had a fair crop, but couldn't thresh, due to a wet fall. We had to leave it and thresh it the next spring.

In the late part of the fall, at the beginning of the month of December, I noticed my cook got a lot stouter and fatter. I thought we'd go Arborg for the winter months. I got my father to look after the chores in Westbourne and we went to Arborg. My sister Martha was going to high school in Westbourne, and she stayed there with my dad. After we arrived in Arborg, I took my cook to a doctor, for there was no doctors in Westbourne, the nearest one being in the town of Portage la Prairie, twenty miles away. The doctor told us that my cook (wife) will be losing some weight, two- or three-weeks time. Despite the hard work she was doing all summer, cooking for seven of us, milking two cows, and laundering on the washboard (for there was no washing machines in those days) but as usual on a farm, she kept on gaining weight.

I couldn't go away too far from home, but in a week's time, the moose hunting season was open. I decided to go with my brother and get a couple of moose. The next morning, we had a guy take us out to the bush with a team of horses, twenty-two miles from home, where I knew there was moose. We took a small tent, and an airtight wood heater, and enough food for about a week. We were in the bush about two p.m. had lunch, fed the horses, and sent the men back home with the horses, and told him to come back in five or six days, and to bring us more food in case we had to stay longer. We got the tent up, and told my brother Mike to get everything ready, and I went in the bush to see if there were any moose tracks. I went out about a mile, and saw a few moose tracks and came back to camp early, because it was December, it was getting dark earlier.

The next morning, we both went out, and we shot a moose before dinner. I left my brother to skin the moose, and I went in alone and about two and a half hours, I got another moose, and skinned that one myself and came back to the tent at dark. Mike was already in the tent, getting supper ready. We had moose liver for supper. When you walk all day hunting, you get very tired. We went to sleep in a bed of hay, but for some reason I only slept about an hour. I couldn't sleep, but was thinking, I should be home. I got up and started dressing. My brother was sleeping and I woke him up and told him I was going home. The first thing he asked me, was, "Are you crazy?" "Why go home now?" "Go to sleep, and get some rest, and go in the morning." I told him, "I didn't know why, but I had a feeling, I should go home." I told him to take care of himself, and if everything is okay, I would be back the next day. I started out for home, about eight thirty p.m. It was a moonlit night. There was a six-mile bush trail that we had made, and then the walking got better, where people had been hailing timber and logs. I got home in about six and a half hours. Everybody was asleep. I knocked on the door and woke my mother up, and she was surprised and happy to see me, as she thought something happened to me in the wild. After I had asked, how everything was, she said, "I think okay, but your wife was complaining a few hours before, she had a lot of pain." I went to a room where my cook (wife) was, and she was extremely glad to see me, but she also asked, "what happened?" she said, she wasn't getting much sleep, as she was having quite a bit of pain. I left her room. Mother gave me a lunch, I was eating and talking with her for awhile. I thought, I would go lay down, but went to see my wife instead, and she was moaning with pain. My mother told me to go and get a doctor. I went out and hitched the horses to a cutter (sleigh) and away I went eight miles to town to find a doctor. The doctor came back with me and around five thirty a.m. we had a baby girl, whom we named Elsie. The next day, I sent a few men to bring Mike and the moose meat back home, and after a week we went out and got one more moose.

Towards the spring, we went back to Westbourne. I worked on the tractor from six a.m. until eleven p.m. until I finished seeding. It was easier for my cook, because she had lost some weight and had a daughter helping her.

That following summer, we had a great crop, but towards harvest time, the weather got wet, and the grain got badly rusted. We cut what we could, but it kept raining, when we started threshing with a big threshing outfit, we had eighteen men to feed. We only threshed about two half days a week, of oats and barley, because it wasn't dry enough to thresh the wheat.

One day, when we were threshing, I was hauling grain and as I got about a quarter mile away from the machine, I looked back, and saw a team of horses with a stock wagon running away. They were coming my way, and I stopped my team of horses and tied the lines to the wagon box, and jumped off my wagon to try and stop the runaway team. They were approaching close on the full gallop, and got me on the wagon pole and the neck yoke, and kept running with me holding on to the pole. I was trying hard to stop them and one horse tumbled over and fell, and I fell under him. The other horse lost its balance and fell on the first horse that was on top of me. I passed out, and was lying under that horse, until the men came running over. They didn't know what happened to me, until they got the horses unhitched, and standing up, and finding me out cold. However, they started working on me, and brought me back to life, I was not able to do anything, and stayed inside, recovering for a week from that fall. We quit threshing, as the weather stayed wet and we planned to thresh, after freezing up. In about three weeks time, it started freezing with rain and snow drifting into the stocks, and we couldn't thresh then, and hoped to get it done the next spring.

During the following winter, it was 1922-1923, when we got a very heavy snowfall, over fifty inches. The trains couldn't go any place without the snowplows ahead of them. The winter was incredibly cold and stayed cold until the middle of April 1923. Suddenly, the south winds came along for a few days, and it was warm and rained heavily. The snow melted like a snow ball in hell, and the whole country was flooded from Riding Mountain to Lake Manitoba. God was good to the poor people and helped them not to worry about threshing, washing away roads and bridges too.

We decided to go on a smaller farm, which was available three miles away, about two weeks time, we decided to move. There was approximately two hundred and forty acres under cultivation on the smaller farm. My father was home in Arborg, and in the fall of 1922, Peter had quit, to go to Winnipeg to take a course in the barbering trade. There was only me, Mike and my wife (I call her cook) and her helper Elsie, who was about seventeen months old. After a couple of days we got most of our machinery moved, and on the 22nd day of April we took two loads of furniture, and while we were loading the furniture, my wife worked like a slave, cleaning the rooms, scrubbing the floors. About noon we arrived at the other place. The first thing we did was unload the cook stove and had it set up for our cook to make lunch. When the things were unloaded, lunch was ready. While we had lunch, the horses were fed, and rested. After lunch, we went back to get the rest of the household items, without setting up beds or furniture before we left. It was all just left on the floor. When we arrived at the old farm, we started to load, when one of our friends, who was also farming four miles south of our place, came over, and told us, that they were quitting farming, as they lost most of their crop. He told me that he was pulling out the next morning at six a.m., and said, I could have about fifty bushels of oats if I wanted, provided I took it away that day. Since we needed feed oats, I decided to take it away. I suggested to my brother Mike, to take what he could, and go and get the things set up in the new house.

I went over to that farmer friend of ours. The road was muddy in places, as it was a clay grade road, and by the time I got the oats loaded, it was already sunset. This guy asked me to come inside and have something to eat. After lunch, I went on my wagon, and started for home. About one hundred yards away from his house, I had to cross a small ditch, on which the bridge had washed away, and I was stuck with my load of grain in that ditch. I went back to his house and asked him to take his team of horses to pull me out, and he did. But by then it was dark, however, the moon was coming up and I thought I would have a moon lit night to drive home in, and he said, "Why drive at night." Unhitch your team and put them in the barn and come and sleep in the house. I'll be getting up at five a.m. so you can go in the daylight, instead of getting stuck again on the road and having to walk home. I was just about to do that, when something came to mind, that I should go home in case brother Mike was late, and he would be working alone and mad at me. I headed out towards home, and it was going well, the horses were enjoying the walk. At about eleven thirty p.m., the moon light was good, and I arrived at the place I was moving from. I looked over and noticed a team of horses and a wagon standing on the road just outside the gate. I stopped my horses and tied the lines and went to see who it was. It was my brother Mike, with the same load. I asked him, what had happened and if he was home, and he said, "How could I go home!" I wanted to take a pair of colts, and tied them behind the wagon, but they won't go, they pull back." I helped him to get to my wagon, and let him go ahead, and I followed with my team, with no trouble at all. I said to him, "Why in the heck did you bother taking the colts, you know they wont walk, you should have left them and gone home." At that moment, I thought of our cook and how she was doing with only a small child in the house. We arrived about one thirty a.m. at the house and noticed that there were no lights on. I rushed inside and found the lamp and lit it and found my wife lying on the floor with one of the mattresses crying with pain. I asked her what happened, and she said she must of being working too much and it seems like I'll be having a baby. I told Mike to light a fire in the stove, as the house was cold already, and I went out and unhitched one of the horses from my wagon and took the harness off. I jumped on his bareback and went to go and get a midwife that I knew was good. There was no telephone, only in town, when I got to her place, I woke her up, and told her what the problem was. She was an elderly woman in her sixties. I asked her husband to give me his buggy, as I came on horse back. He was a big fellow, slow as molasses at Christmas time, and after we got out, he couldn't find a harness to fit my horse. We finally found some harness traces and we tied them around my horse's neck. I let the old lady in the buggy and I ran along side of the horse, as close as I could, which was a good mile and a half. when I got to the house, I was sweating buckets. When we arrived at the house, my brother Mike shouted!! "Oh no, you are too late!!" I nearly dropped dead, but the old lady said, "What do you mean??" Mike said, "I helped her, and she had the baby!!" That was our baby boy we named John.

After a couple of weeks, we settled on a smaller farm, and started working on the fields, and had about one hundred and fifty acres of crops in. During the summer, we had a couple of small jobs, on the roads, fixing bridges and washed-out grades. It kept us living, but at harvest time, I had to buy twine and tractor fuel, and that got me into more debt.

After threshing, grain prices declined again, and wheat was down to forty-eight cents a bushel, barley, twenty-eight cents, and oats, eighteen cents. After selling what wheat we had, and it paid for the threshing and grocery bills. We had about one hundred dollars for each of us, dad, Mike and me. I gave my dad, one hundred dollars to go home with. And Mike and I, stayed on the farm.

I bought a dozen small pigs, and planned to raise them on the barley we had, instead of selling the barley at about twenty- eight cents a bushel. We fed about forty-five pigs and some poultry.

We crushed six hundred and fifty of barley and fed almost all of that to the pigs. When the pigs were about ready for market; the price went down on them too. We shipped forty of them, and got twelve dollars a pig, which is about six cents a pound. We didn't make much money again. During the winter, I was lucky to get a job on the C.N.R. track, shoveling snow and building snow fences, and in my spare time, I was trapping weasels and squirrels. Weasels were around a dollar a pelt, and squirrels brought five cents and they helped pull us through the winter without getting into more debt.

The following summer, we kept on farming, and the price on grain improved somewhat in the spring, but soon as the farmers started threshing, down the prices went again. It was all handled through the grain exchange, and the government had no control then. It was like now adays with price rising on everything that poor people must buy. The grain we sold, that fall, we got three hundred dollars between the three of us. About one hundred and twenty dollars each for a whole summers work. That fall, we had a new member to the family, a baby born in the late part of October 1924.

There were a lot of farmers quitting farming, so I quit too. During the winter we prepared everything for sale in spring. About the beginning of April, we advertised to have an auction sale of farm machinery and livestock in April. In the middle of April, we had a two-day snow storm, and had about twenty inches of snow fall. After a week, the weather was very warm again, and in a couple of days, the snow was gone, but the water from the melt laid over the fields and the roads, making it difficult for the sale. Not many came and everything went dirt cheap. After the sale, we did not have enough money to pay our debts, and we had no place to go. Mike went back to Arborg, and I moved in to a C.N.R. bunkhouse, which was like a box car partitioned into three rooms, eight by ten in size.

We lived there, about two months, and I got a job operating a tractor on a farm, at sixty dollars a month. I worked for five months and made three hundred dollars that summer, almost as much as the three of us had made on the farm, farming for ourselves. The next summer, another baby boy came to our family, and that was Bill (William).

During the following winter, I worked on the railroad again (spare time only) and I started trapping wolves, and skunks. The price was good, as some wolve skins, I sold for twenty-five dollars. I made over three hundred dollars over the winter.

That summer, it was very hot living in the box car (bunkhouse), so I rented a three-room house, which was available near that railroad siding (section yard) by the name of Cowdor. Bill, my son was born in that house. We were paying fifteen dollars a month rent, and I made a little money that winter and decided to buy the house. Towards the spring, I bought the house at Cowdor for five hundred dollars.

The following summer, I got a job, on the railroad, as a section labourer. I was earning eighty- five dollars a month. After working one summer, I was laid off for the winter, like the rest of the men. During the winter, I trapped again, but it was not very good, and I had to work odd jobs, when the opportunity came.

One day, I went to the town of Westbourne for my mail and a man asked me if I could come give him a hand to operate a tractor to do some grain crushing. His name was Dr. Hartford. He was an American who had quit doctoring, came to Canada and had bought a section of land (640 acres) with the buildings and started to livestock ranch. He had cattle, sheep, pigs, and raised grain for his own use. He was the doctor who brought our son William into this world, which was a very serious case, as I had to get another doctor from Portage la prairie, and I couldn't refuse him, and never asked how much he would pay. I told him I would come the next morning at six a.m. It was very cold, twenty below zero, and I had to walk five miles. I arrived at his place at eight a.m. And they were just getting up at that time. He called me in, and told me to wait until he was dressed. Then he went out, and fed the cattle and horses, then went back to the house for breakfast. He told me to take a shovel, and showed me where his old titan tractor was under the bush, covered in snow. I could only see a little of the hind wheels which were about five feet high. I went and dug it out and got some hay and set fire to it to warm the tractor up, started it, then dug a road to take it out to the yard where we were going to crush the grain. When I got it to the granary, he called me for dinner. After dinner, we crushed grain until sunset. After sunset, we fed the pigs, sheep and cattle, then went for supper around six p.m. After supper he asked me, how much he owed me. I said, "You know, I worked hard all day, and we only stopped for one meal at noon, and I hope you are satisfied for what we have done. He then said "Oh yes, I am satisfied." He says, "How about seventy-five cents?" and I said, "Well if you think that's all it's worth, I have no say, as the job is already done."

But his wife said, "Oh dad, give the man a dollar." So, he gave me a dollar for my twelve-hours work. He was heading to town, and got a ride with him in the horse cutter and walked the other two miles home. It was after eight p.m. when I got home, over fourteen hours from the time I left home for one dollar and I worked like a slave.

We made it through that winter, and didn't make much money, but in the spring, I jumped on the railroad section again, on the same line, but ten miles west of what they called Lakeland. The difference was, I had to do my own cooking, and came home once a week, and Sunday evening or early Monday morning, I had to go back, to be there at eight a.m. I used to come by what they called hand car on the railroad track. If there was no wind, or you travelled with the wind, it wasn't too bad. I made about seven to eight miles per hour, but going against the wind it was very hard to make five miles an hour. I used to take from home, baked bread, and some other food that would keep a couple or three days, as there were no fridges or hydro out in the country. We always had ice stored for the summer supply where we kept our food, but the milk was the hardest to keep, because when it thundered and stormed, it would turn sour right away, and then, we had to use can milk.

After a couple of months, I decided to buy a car. I went to Portage one Saturday night, and bought one, a Chevrolet 490 model, which I found out later, was the worst car on the market. I only paid one hundred and twenty dollars for it. And during the dry weather, when the roads were good, it always took me home and back to work. During the harvest I used to stook grain for the farmers around thirty cents an acre. If the crop wasn't heavy, I averaged two acres an hour, so I made a few extra dollars after six p.m., but that only lasted a couple of weeks. Some days, we used to go to a neighbouring farmer, and help them milk cows, do the chores, and I got a quart of milk for the porridge, which we cooked every day, as there was no ready made (cooked) cereals like now.

After freezing up, I got home, with the promise that I'd be a steady section employee in the following year, on the Embury section between Langruth and Amaranth. The same line, but further north. It was about thirty miles away from home, and I would have to batch.

Towards the winter, I worked all over, and paid off my debts. And paid for my sister Kate five hundred dollars, that all three of us borrowed. After they left me to pay all that, I also paid for the house. I was glad that I didn't owe anyone money, and we had some poultry, which we had for our own use, and I bought another cow for the winter milk supply, because in previous winters, I had to go half a mile at seven a.m. to a farmer to buy milk for the children.

The following spring, I wasn't well. I went to portage to see a doctor, who told me that I had congestion in my chest, which had been caused by the runaway horses, that ran over me a couple of years. After the doctor treated it, I felt better, and when a job was available on the section, I got a call to work on the track near home. I worked about two months, and I started feeling sick again, in the chest, I was especially bothered when tamping the ties, always bending down. I didn't know what to do. One day, I received a letter from Arborg, one of my sisters wrote that my father was sick and getting worse, almost all winter with a pain in his arm, between his elbow, and shoulder, it was swollen. I took a few days off my job, and I went to Arborg, and took my father to see a doctor in Winnipeg, who told us he had sarcoma which is cancer. In the meantime, I saw the doctor about myself, and he told me to quit the job.

The doctor told my dad, that they would have to amputate his arm, which upset him very much and he refused the operation. The doctor told him that if he didn't have it amputated, he would only have about a year to live, and about eleven and a half months later, my father passed away.

After taking dad back to Arborg, and on my way back home I had to see the doctor about myself, and I called in to J.R Watkins products and made an inquiry to see if I could peddle the products. I had all the particulars on the product and went home to tell my wife, what the doctor had suggested, and she was very upset, and didn't want me to go into debt again, as I needed three hundred and fifty to four hundred dollars, to start the Watkins business. It didn't matter what I told her, she insisted that I hold onto the job until we had some money of our own.

I decided I would try for a couple of months and borrowed two hundred dollars from my section foremen, who was a single man at the time, and I asked him for a leave of absence. I made a box like a trunk to fit in the backseat of my car, as it had only side curtains, no glass windows. Then I went to Winnipeg, and talked to the credit manager of J.R. Watkins, and got a five hundred dollar order with a four hundred down payment and I started out peddling house to house.

I didn't know anybody; my district was north of Gladstone of the west side of Lake Manitoba and far north, sixty miles. The first few days, I was excited, but eventually got use to the people, and how to approach them. And a month of travel, I made a few more dollars than I had made while working on the section, the only difference being that during the winter I had to use horses and some trips took me a month away from home without hearing what was going on as you were in a different place every day, and there were no telephones to be able to get in touch with home.

In the winter, it was hard to get a place to stay over night with horses. I remember, one night on the first trip I made to Kinosota P.O. I went about two miles after dark and called at about eight places before I got a place for my team horses. I was getting hungry, my team was tired and the weather was getting cold along Lake Winnipeg. Most people were Metis that lived in small log shacks.

After I found the place, and I got my horses in the stable, we got to the house and the fellow said they had no bed for me, but I could sleep on the couch, which was made from lumber and sitting under the stairs. This was a log house with only one room, but it had an upstairs room, where the family slept. The stairs were built with narrow steps, like a step ladder. They were a large family with six or seven children.

They asked me if I was hungry, I said I was hungry and they invited me to a supper of fish, Bannock, and tea, no bread, no pudding nor pie. If it was today, I would tell them goodbye. After supper, we talked for awhile then the man said anytime I wanted to go to bed I should. He went up stairs with the older children and I laid down on the couch.

It had fish netting for a mattress, and a horse blanket. I had my own horse blankets, which I used as a quilt. After I laid down, the rest of the kids started going upstairs, and the lady was carrying the smaller children upstairs too. As I looked up, I had to turn my head to the side, for she had no pants or bloomers on. I slept well, as you do, after being out in the cold. In the morning, the man was up before daylight. I looked up and asked him, what time it was, and he said, "he didn't know, as they had no clock. He lit a coal oil lamp, and I looked at my watch, and it was seven a.m. he told me, not to rush, that he would feed the horses, but I got up anyways. After a short while, his wife came down with the children, they had to go to school. She started cooking breakfast, and had a cast iron frying pan out, and cooked porridge in it. She poured porridge from each one of them, as there were four kids at the table. Then she started cooking in another frying pan, and started to give me the bowl of the first child who had the least porridge from the first pan, and then the other started to howl, "Mama, I want more porridge!!" he kept saying, "Wait Johnny boy, wait, I will give you more porridge." I don't know how many frying pans she used, but her husband came down and asked for porridge. I told her, "I don't eat porridge." Just looking in that pan, was enough for me. So, he had his porridge, and I had tea and a piece of Bannock. I tried not to be there at night, after that.

In the spring, I bought myself a half ton ford truck, so I could haul more stuff. During the summer, I decided to move out of Cowder (Westbourne) into my territory, so that I wouldn't travel too far. My wife did not want to move, and hoped I would quit peddling, and go back on the railroad section to work again.

I tried to move to Amaranth, where there was one old man by the name of Bob, who had a little store where Mr. Parsons is now. But Bob kept putting it off. I heard that another man in Alonsa, had a small store. The poor fellow was sick and had to quit the business. I made plans to buy his stock, but rented the building. I persuaded my wife to move with hopes that she might look after what was in the store. There was only five hundred and sixty dollars worth of stock, mostly surplus stuff. We moved into Alonsa in September 1930.

The store building was 24x 34 feet, with a flat roof. It had a lean to it at the back, which was 12x24 with a flat roof. It was about six feet at the low end of the building, and was used as a warehouse.

I couldn't find a house to live in with my family, we moved to that shanty with our six kids. We only had a small room for one bed, and the kids slept on the floor. After we got settled, I kept peddling and tried to collect most of the bills in which I had a few hundred dollars outstanding. Towards the winter, I got more stock for the store, and showed my wife how to sell, and look after customers, as I already had a little experience. I worked until the winter was heavy, and then I stayed home. With what little stuff we had, we made a living.

The following spring, I bought a few head of cattle, and peddled for a couple of months, and then the depression came. R.B. Bennet's Conservation Party brought the depression, which was the worst in the history of Canada. There was no work for any body, and those that did work, had to work for very low wages. Five-ten-fifteen dollars a month. Thousands and thousands of people were in the soup kitchens through out Canada.

Business got very tough, and grain prices were down. Wheat, was forty-five cents a bushel, barley twenty-five cents, and oat, fifteen cents. Livestock was down too, to two cents a pound. Butter was five cents a pound, but axle grease was seven cents a pound. Eggs were three cents a dozen. I remember very well, getting eighty-one cents for a thirty-dozen crate of eggs. I was also buying cattle. I bought twenty-seven head for one hundred and twenty-eight dollars, and shipped them to Winnipeg. I received one hundred and twenty-two dollars, I lost six dollars on a carload of cattle, but I figured that I made money, because most of it was on the store bill and trade.

After, about three years, I decided to buy old shacks (store buildings) and I sold my house in Cowder, and bought the store buildings in Alonsa, and decided to build a house behind the store on the same lot. Labour was cheap, and so was building material. I hired a few men, most of whom were working on their store accounts, and we build a five-room house, three rooms down, two up. We then, had another girl, named Stella, then we had seven children. We finished the outside walls and the roof and we moved into that house, and I kept working on the inside, myself all winter, mostly at night until I had it finished. Then I decided to go into the Massey Harris Implement business. I had some lumber on trade and built a warehouse and flour and feed shack. I got the Robin Hood Flour Agency. The following year, we had another baby boy named Martin. The same year, I bought another lot with a stable on it and as the kids were getting bigger, we milked ten to twelve cows. It was hard to look after keeping cattle in town, when I had a change, I bought a quarter section of land (150 acres) and got it fenced in, dug a well and moved the cattle there. It was one and a half miles from town, it wasn't handy for the kids to go and milk the cows. Therefore, I built a small shack, and stable during the summer, we let them stay there overnight and we told them whatever they made milking cows, would be their spending money.

The first summer they did very well. There was three of them, if I remember correctly, Elsie, John, and Russel milking eight to ten cows. They shipped two cans of cream a week, and we used a lot of milk and cream. They were getting eighty-two cents to eighty-seven cents for a three gallon can of cream, which was a dollar sixty-five to a dollar seventy-five a week, between them, to give each, experience and value of money.

About 1935, the cattle price improved a little, and I sold most of the cattle, and bought another quarter section of land, adjacent to the one I had. Some of it was cultivated, and the following year we put in a crop, so we would have our own livestock feed.

The following year, I built a house on the farm, and in the fall, the war broke out, the second world war. Everything started to go up, and most young men, were drafted to go to war.

In January 1941, I took a load of cattle to Winnipeg with my son John in the truck, as he was driving a truck for Alonsa Transfer. We stayed overnight in Winnipeg. The next morning, I got up, had coffee and toast, and was getting ready to go into the city to do my business. Just as I had my overcoat on, I felt like I wanted to sneeze. I sneezed rather hard and loud, and was paralyzed in my left arm. I had stayed over night with my wife's sister and her mother-in-law, they were very scared, for I fainted several times before the doctor arrived at the house. When the doctor came in, he couldn't do anything, nor could he get me into the hospital, because the hospitals were filled with young army men and women. And it seemed like every soldier and every woman in the city of Winnipeg were sick.

John was called to the city the same month. Mother (wife) could not come to see me for about a week. The doctor was coming to the house where I was lying sick, and at the same time, hoping they would be able to put me in a hospital, but without results. Mother (wife) hired a car in Alonsa and came to Winnipeg and took me home, where I stayed a month before I could get to a hospital in Portage La Prairie. I stayed in the hospital at Portage La Prairie for five weeks and then I got a little better. I was able to walk on crutches.

When I left the hospital in Portage, I stayed home about a month, and then I was able to get into the Winnipeg General Hospital. I stayed there for seven weeks and didn't get much better. Two years later, I went to the Mayo Clinic in Rochester, Minnesota, where they really helped me. Six months later, I started walking without crutches. And thanks to God, I was walking for most of my life.

In the meantime, Elsie got married and moved on the farm, where I built a five-room house. I built a new store building and business started getting good. During the war, everything was booming. I built another building for farm implements, and we bought another farm adjacent in town, and built a house on it.

Then, John came home from Germany. "Thank God, he was not wounded." He took over the oil and implement business and Elsie and her husband Walter decided to go into the hotel business. The old hotel in Alonsa was for sale, and they decided to buy it. Since, they didn't have enough money, they persuaded us to go with them in partnership, which we did. Mother and I decided to sell the store, and we did, then went into the hotel business. Mother and Walter, were beer waiters.

My sister Elsie and sister Stella were cooks and waitresses, and I was a Joe Boy and tried to help where help was needed.

A year later, Elsie and Walter decided to quit the hotel business, for it was too rough on them and the hours were long. They started a restaurant business in Amaranth, mother and I, took over the hotel. Since we didn't know the ins and outs of the hotel business, you know its like the old saying goes, "Its not what you know, but who you know." And we didn't know the liquor inspectors or we could have tipped them, but instead, they condemned our hotel building and forced us to build a new one. There was another strain and big worry, as we had no other money. By the time we got everything prepared, summer went by and the following spring we started to build a new hotel. That was 1950. One morning, as we were digging out the basement, I had a slight heart attack. The doctor ordered me to keep away from work, so our son John took it over and my other son's Bill and Russell, helped all they could. Russell got married and lived on the farm, and Bill was a teacher in school. In November, we moved into a new twelve room hotel, a fully modern building and a thirty-thousand-dollar debt. John helped a lot in the hotel, when he wasn't busy in the implement shop, and mother looked after the parlour as a beer waiter.

John quit the implement and oil business and went away to work for the greyhound Bus Lines and stayed with them for a long time. Mother, Stella, and I kept the hotel business until 1959, until we sold it for fifty thousand dollars. The same building was sold in September of 1970 for ninety-six thousand dollars, with some improvements and a ladies parlor added.

We paid our debts, and paid a little to the boys, for helping us, as mother wasn't feeling good anymore, we retired. We moved to Winnipeg, to our house, which was part of the deal on the hotel. After I moved to Winnipeg, I built a garage and rumpus room in the basement, and lived there until the good lord came.

'Dido's last words of thought'

Despite stride and struggle, we are proud and ecstatic to know this country, called Canada. For what it is, for our children, grandchildren, and great grandchildren, so they don't have to suffer, and go hungry like we did, and hope they will be able to maintain the good of this country, and improve it for the future of their children. Since they have more education, and a better start with more technical facilities to frustrate everything that is not progressive for the people, and their country, including the old political liars, who have been fooling the poor people for over a century. There is no reason, to have poor and unemployed people in this country, nor hungry people in this world. There is no reason for killing and massacring the poor and hungry people when they demand food, especially in their own country. Let them settle their own problems, instead of children going there to kill them, and helping the rich millionaires. Since the lords' commands are "Thou shall not kill" we must obey them and not ignore them. If we want to be proper Christians, we must stop killing each other – Amen.

Made in United States
North Haven, CT
03 June 2024

53265231R00033